Beyond
the
Door

Entering Into a Relationship of Oneness with God

R H O N D A   A M B R O S E

WESTBOW°
PRESS
A DIVISION OF THOMAS NELSON
& ZONDERVAN

WestBow Press books may be ordered through booksellers or by contacting:

WestBow Press
A Division of Thomas Nelson & Zondervan
1663 Liberty Drive
Bloomington, IN 47403
www.westbowpress.com
1 (866) 928-1240

ISBN: 978-1-4908-6520-1 (sc)
ISBN: 978-1-4908-6521-8 (hc)
ISBN: 978-1-4908-6519-5 (e)

Library of Congress Control Number: 2015901393

Print information available on the last page.

WestBow Press rev. date: 02/18/2015

$\mathcal{C}$ONTENTS

Introduction vii

Chapter 1 Soaking …What in the World Is That? 1
Chapter 2 Why Read the Bible? 9
Chapter 3 Cultivating a Secret Life with God 17
Chapter 4 Your Mouth Is Enormously Potent 27
Chapter 5 Knowing Who You Are 37
Chapter 6 A Blank Canvas 45
Chapter 7 In Process 51
Chapter 8 Living Victorious 57
Chapter 9 Dating God 65
Chapter 10 It's All about Love! 71

Bread Crumbs (Resources) 81

INTRODUCTION

Something very powerful begins to happen within each of us when we are wooed by love. We are not only born with an innate need to be loved; we are created specifically and intentionally for it. In Hosea 2:16 God says,

> But now I am going to woo her—I will bring her
> out to the desert and I will speak to her heart.
> (CJB)

The same verse in the NIV: "Therefore I am now going to allure her; I will lead her into the desert and speak tenderly to her." The Greek/Hebrew meaning for *woo* is: "accept, acquiesce in; authorize; be in agreement with; give ones approval."

There is an interesting story in the Bible (Judges 19) that tells an account of a woman who is *outside* her master's house where she is repeatedly abused and collapses in death with her hands on the threshold. While the circumstances of my spiritual journey are unlike this woman's, I too lay dying on the threshold, just outside the very thing I was created for—a relationship of oneness with Father God.

I had accepted Jesus as my Savior, attended church with my family on Sundays, was engaged in a Bible study class on Wednesday nights, and I sang in the choir; yet I was unhappy, unfulfilled, and felt powerless. Until one day in a moment of raw, blunt honesty, I said to God, "If this is as good as it gets, it is not enough!"

I know now that it was His great love for me that was wooing me to Him, drawing me into the *more* that I was craving—into His world, into a friendship beyond the threshold of salvation, and into a journey of intimacy and relationship, into the ecstasy of *knowing Him*. He led me across the threshold by dropping what I refer to as a trail of bread crumbs in the form of a variety of individuals, books, CDs, etc., that I began to pick up and apply one by one. As I began to put into practice the revelation, knowledge, and understanding that He was giving me through these bread crumbs, they enabled me to stand and begin the process of walking through the door and into the wholeness of His love. Salvation is essential and leads us into a glorious eternal life with God. But it is also designed to be an entrance into experiencing fullness with God here on earth—*now.* I discovered that everything I need or desire is wrapped up in the gift of knowing Him. Everything *you* need or desire is wrapped up in the gift of knowing Him.

My hope is that by sharing how I stepped through the door, how I began to know His nature and cultivate our relationship it will encourage you as well to cross over and experience firsthand the life-altering power of being overwhelmed by His love and experiencing the peace and joy of knowing Him and then to know Him more and more and more!

You were absolutely created to live in the life-altering reality of what Jesus prayed in John 17:3 TPT.

Eternal life means to know and experience You
As the only true God,
And to know and experience Jesus Christ,
As the Son whom you have sent.

The bread crumbs He provides for you may be different from mine, but hopefully these will give you a grid or a starting point from which to launch into your own personal journey of walking through the door …

     … into His love
     … into His goodness
     … into knowing Him.

CHAPTER 1

Soaking …What in the World Is That?

The word *soak* in a dictionary is defined as "make or allow (something) to become thoroughly wet by immersing it in liquid; become saturated by immersion; to penetrate or affect the mind or feelings."

Words synonymous with *soak* include *immerse, steep, marinate,* and *submerge.*

Being from the South, when I read these definitions, my mind immediately goes to "pickling." This is the process that a small cucumber goes through to become a pickle. One simply immerses the cucumber in vinegar (or a similar solution) and allows it to marinate until it is completely saturated. Keep in mind that the cucumber is not doing anything during this process; it is simply resting, soaking. What it is immersed *in* is doing the work.

We need to learn how to just *be* with God. Rest in Him. Soaking is a great way to gear down from all the activities and concerns of the day and just chill with Holy Spirit. Our spirits, our minds, and our bodies need this. And yes, it may feel like a waste of time as you begin to practice, but oh how wonderfully productive soaking is!

Soaking is not praying, it is not praising, it is not asking, and it is not talking. It is lying there connecting with Abba (Father) God. Soaking is taking time to rest in His presence and allowing His love to saturate us. It is a doorway into intimacy with God.

This gearing down did not come easily for me at first. I would lie down to soak, and my mind would flood with all the things I needed to do! So I simply kept a paper and pen handy and would write down a list of the things that came to mind until I could lie there, in rest, and focus on Him. Soon, I found myself not needing a list at all but being able to lie down, rest, connect, and marinate. I began to feel His presence and hear from Him like never before.

Many times in the New Testament, we read how Jesus modeled this for us. The Bible tells us that He "went away" to spend time with the Father. This was not a casual thing that He did when He had nothing else to do. He purposely and intentionally took time away from everything and everyone to be alone with His Father. He would get up hours before the disciples and steal away with Abba. If Jesus needed time alone with God, how much more do we?

You can soak in silence, you can sing your own love song to Him, or you can listen to music while you soak. I mostly use music that is calm and soothing. Often, I have music without words; other times, words without music; and sometimes, I rock out!

Finding a quiet place free of distraction may take some creative thinking. When I first began to soak, I had two middle school children who were very active in sports, and my husband and I worked full-time jobs. When and where would I find the time and place to soak?

Here is how I started: I decided to get up twenty minutes earlier than normal and try this soaking thing out. My laundry room became my soaking spot, partly because it is the farthest room from the bedrooms of my still-sleeping family and is the room most likely to be avoided. I placed a blanket on the floor, had my pen and paper handy, hit play on my CD player, turned down the lights, spread myself down, and focused my attention on Him. My only desire in this was simply to *know Him*. I had read about experiences and encounters that others have had in His presence, and I wanted to experience Him myself firsthand.

Nothing seemed to be happening after soaking for twenty minutes. I felt nothing. I decided I would thank Him for His time and tell Him that I would be back tomorrow. After a short time, things began to happen. I began to feel His presence like liquid love being poured on and inside of me. I was hooked! My twenty minutes increased to thirty, forty, and then an hour. Sometimes, all I could do was cry. Other times, I would lie there with a huge smile. And there were still times that I didn't feel much at all.

I began to notice that on the days I did not particularly feel anything happening, I would find myself in a situation at work or with my family that required a wise solution, and out of my mouth would come this profound, productive answer that would surprise me. What came out was better than what I could have come up with, and later I would walk around the corner and tell God, "You made me look really good!" I knew that while I was soaking, God just deposited what He knew I would need. It was like the scene in the movie *The Matrix* when they are sitting in the chair plugged in. Whatever they needed was simply downloaded into them. As we "plug" into God, He downloads to us what He knows we need!

So many things happen when you soak. You are being immersed in Him, and that causes change! Remember the cucumber soaking in vinegar? It is being totally changed inside and out on its way to becoming a pickle. So are we being changed inside and out as we soak in Him. While you soak, He may bring to your mind something you need to deal with or something that you need forgiveness for. Maybe there is someone you need to forgive so that you can be free. He may heal wounds from your past. He may touch you emotionally. He may heal you physically, comfort you, or refresh you. He may awaken creative gifts that are dormant within you. He will be for you what you need, even when you yourself are unsure what that is. Yes, God is that good!

Accept and receive the fact that God is totally and unconditionally in love with you!

> Before I shaped you in the womb, I knew all about you. Before you saw the light of day I had holy plans for you. (Jeremiah 1:5 *The Message*)

> Long before He laid down earth's foundation, He had us in mind, had settled on us the focus of His love, to be made whole and holy by His love. Long, long ago He decided to adopt us into His family through Jesus Christ. (Ephesians 1:4–5 *The Message*)

This means that God knows every single detail about each one of us—the good, the bad, and even the ugly—yet He chose us. So I get to be loved by Him … just as I am! He doesn't choose us out of obligation either but out of delight! In Zephaniah 3:17b (NKJV) we read,

> He will rejoice over you with gladness, He will quiet you with His love, He will rejoice over you with singing.

Knowing this allows us to ask Him anything and everything because He is interested in each of us and delights in being with us! And even if I happen to fall asleep while soaking, I don't have to feel guilty. He will hold me while I sleep, knowing that my spirit is always active!

You are unique, and your soaking experience will be as well!

Soaking is like paving a landing strip of invitation for God to come. Allowing yourself to marinate in God's unconditional love will begin to change you. Receiving God's love creates a capacity for us to return the love He so freely gives us back to Him.

CHAPTER 2

Why Read the Bible?

One thing that encourages me to read the Bible every day is knowing that it is *alive* and *active*! It is the voice of truth that I get to live *from*, my true north that points me to Him regardless of what any given day may bring.

As we go about our days, lots of things can land on us, such as disappointment, a harsh or negative word spoken over us, or a lie whispered from the Enemy. Many things happen to and around us daily, but as we read His Word, it gently washes over us and removes those things that are not good, even things we aren't aware of, just like standing under a waterfall washes away dirt from our body.

> Husbands, love your wives, just as Christ also loved the church, and gave Himself for her, that He might sanctify and cleanse her with the washing of water by the Word.
>
> (Ephesians 5:25–26 NKJV)

If something like disappointment sits on us long enough, we will turn toward it and focus our attention on it. What we focus on, we empower, whether it is positive or negative. Reading His Word washes Enemy fodder away so our focus remains on Jesus. When we focus on Jesus, we empower Him to be alive and active in our everyday lives.

As I read His Word, I get to know Him, His nature, His ways, and His voice.

I don't read Scripture with the goal of understanding everything I am reading. I read Scripture to *know Him.* In learning to know Him, He reveals understanding of what I am reading.

Reading the Bible is all about cultivating a relationship with *Him.*

I read my Bible out loud, if at all possible, so that my own ears can hear His Words. Romans 10:17 gives us this brilliant information,

> So then faith comes by hearing and hearing by
> the word of God. (NKJV)

Faith will come from my hearing Him … my hearing Him will come from the message of Christ in His Word! When we read the Bible, there is a multitude of things going on that we may not be aware of. Just because you do not feel His presence or receive an amazing revelation, His Word is still *active* and there is *always* something taking place from spending time with Him.

Knowing that alone creates a desire in me to want to be with Him, and it opens me up to receive revelation, which one could also call secret messages from Him. Each of us needs to have a secret life with God. He is our safe place, He never leaves us, and His love is unconditional. A secret life with God is the key to the door of our deepest dreams and our deepest desires. For me, reading the Bible is like going on a date with my best friend! When I open His Word, it's like opening a door into another realm, another world that feels like a warm, cozy *home* … yet is like nothing I have ever encountered! Experiences filled with adventures of learning to do things in a radical, new way … His way, and finding that I am having the time of my life in the process!

I *need* His Word. Reading His Word: roots me and enmeshes me with Him, washes darkness off of me, nourishes me, leads me, encourages me, corrects me, intrigues me, speaks to me, tells me secrets, fills me, infuses me, changes me, empowers me, feeds me!

Think about it, we don't go days without eating food for our bodies, why would we ever want to go a day without feeding our spirit! For example: if you have an issue or situation and you don't know what to do, read the book of Psalms until you come across what you are feeling or experiencing—it's in there! If you need wisdom or advice, read Proverbs; it is a recipe for a happy, fulfilled life. In fact, a great way to absorb the wisdom infused within the book of Proverbs is to simply read one chapter a day, each month. There are thirty-one chapters so if you forget a day, no worries. Look at the day on the calendar and simply read that chapter and continue from there. Every time you read it you will discover something new that will help you to live a joyful and victorious life. The Bible is His story, and as we experience it firsthand, we realize just how intentional and purposeful His heart is toward us!

Reading His Word allows us to know what He is like, experience His presence and cultivate relationship with the one who loves us the most, dances with delight over us, and is totally our biggest fan! And we have Holy Spirit, who guides us in all things! Invite Holy Spirit to come and join you as you read; He is the best instructor on the planet, superb at helping each of us understand what we are reading and applying what we learn into everyday life.

Experiencing God changes everything, and as you get to know Him you will discover that He is fun! He is a hoot. He tells jokes, loves to laugh, and totally enjoys engaging with you! In fact, He is more fun than we are. We are all serious most of the time—worried with what to do, how to do it, and then how to pay for it. He, on the other hand, knows full well what to do, how to do it, and He owns the universe.

His Word is a huge key in knowing Him. Knowing Him is the most fun-filled adventure possible to mankind!

For those of you who grew up with the King James Version as I did, it is easy to appreciate the beautiful and poetic way it is worded; I just didn't understand a lot of what I was reading. The

Amplified Bible helped me understand what I was reading by breaking down the words and giving me additional information that enabled me to grasp more of what was being said.

I spent a year or so in the NIV Bible, and I would refer to the *Amplified Bible* and often a Bible concordance when I read a verse or phrase that I did not understand. The Message Bible awakened a whole new love for the Bible and for Him! It translates Scripture into everyday language that is simple, bold, and, for me, life altering! The Charles Williams translation of the New Testament is a treasure, revealing His love for me on a deeper level than ever, which caused me to fall deeper in love with Him.

The Voice Bible is what I am currently reading and absolutely loving! I felt God leading me to reread the Old Testament, which for me was always more of a struggle than the New Testament, mostly because I found it difficult to keep up with whom was speaking. *The Voice Bible* actually lists who is speaking, and to whom, which makes reading the Bible more like a history book. It is *His*tory, and it is allowing me to understand verses and phrases that I have just not understood before. It has revealed to me His heart and the heart, motives, and experiences of individuals, which paints a picture of their relationship and intimacy with God. I'm also reading *The Passion Translation of Proverbs*, and it is rocking my world! Reading, listening, and meditating on His Word continually woos me deeper into His love, which expands my capacity and ability to love others.

Now, you certainly don't have to have multiple versions of the Bible in order to have a relationship with God! I was simply intrigued one day by a speaker named Winnie Banov who shared her love for different versions of the Bible at a conference, and that love for the Word somehow smeared me! She has many versions on her website that might also intrigue and interest you!

The Word is alive, and it will alter your day; it will alter your life!

If you don't have a Bible, get one and read it! Listed above are some of the many versions available. You can even download a Bible app or audio Bible for your phone or mobile device, and you can find Bibles online, many that are free of charge.

If you don't enjoy reading the Bible you have, get a different one!

CHAPTER 3

Cultivating a Secret Life with God

In the movie *Superman*, Clark Kent lived on earth, but he was from another planet called Krypton. Clark lived, to most people, as a normal man, but as we all know he had a secret life. When Clark was in need, he would steal away and go to his father.

Makes one wonder if this movie was a spinoff of the gospels and Jesus was the inspiration for the lead character! Jesus came as a normal man, but oh did He have a secret life. His desire to get alone with Father God wasn't only out of need; it was also out of pleasure.

We get to be like Jesus, having a secret life, stealing away to be with Father God!

> And the Holy Spirit came down upon Him in bodily form as a dove, and a voice came out of heaven, You are my Son, my Beloved! In you I am delighted.
>
> (Luke 3:22 *Williams Translation*)

Like I said, we get to be like Jesus, the Holy Spirit comes down upon us, God calls us beloved, and He is totally delighted in us!

Because of Jesus, we go about our normal lives on earth while at the same time being connected with the power of heaven. He comes to live in us; we become His temple (dwelling place).

The commentary in *The Voice Bible* refers to His temple as "the nexus between heaven and earth." We are His temple, His nexus, which means we are the connection or the point of contact that brokers heaven to earth.

> The Spirit of the Lord is upon Me, because He has anointed Me to preach the gospel to the poor; He has sent Me to heal the brokenhearted, to proclaim liberty to the captives and recovery of sight to the blind, to set at liberty those who are oppressed; to proclaim the acceptable year of the Lord. (Luke 4:18–19 NKJV)

God's Word is full of instructions on how we can cultivate a secret life with God. Invite the Holy Spirit to come and help you incorporate God's advice, identity, and nature into your everyday life. Here are some of the specific ways we can do that.

Thankfulness

"Come face-to-face with God, and give thanks."

—Psalm 95:2 *The Voice*

Understanding the many benefits of living with a thankful heart is massive! Not only is it the way we enter into His gates, it causes us to live a life of awareness to the beauty and awe that is in us, in others, in nature, and in everything all around us.

Often we do not *feel* thankful, but as we purposefully begin to speak out something we are thankful for, it begins to shift or move us *into* genuine heartfelt thanks! Even if we start with "Thank you, Jesus, for eyes that see, for a roof over my head, or for the ability to play a sport." Start with what you can give thanks for on any given day, and it will lead to deeper things to be thankful for, even amazed over!

If you find yourself stuck and it seems you have nothing to be thankful for, begin to thank Him for the things He does for you that you are not aware of. Thankfulness leads us into praise, which leads us into worship and intimacy with Him.

> Enter with the password: Thank you! Make yourselves at home, talking praise. Thank Him. Worship Him. (Psalm 100:4 *The Message*)

For a believer, being thankful is like breathing air—we don't get very far without it.

Adoration

Adoration is the act of voicing the awe of God back to Him from the entirety of your being. We read in Psalm 34 of David magnifying the Lord, and we read in Revelations 4 that the angels are constantly surrounding Him with worship and adoration, but until recently I had never actually had someone model adoration.

I had reached a point in my journey with God that I simply ached to know Him more; not from a place of lack or need but from pure desire. God answered that ache by giving me a model of adoration by means of a CD by Bob Hartley.

After soaking to this CD for several days, I began to adore God from my own heart, in my own unique words, and the more I adored Him, the deeper my love for Him grew. I began to incorporate adoring God into my day. The more I adored Him, the more of Him I found myself in awe of.

As I adore Him, I experience and receive love on a new level and find myself refreshed in the process. Adoration takes us beyond our needs, beyond our wants, and allows us to intimately encounter God as we pour out our deepest affections on Him solely because of *who* He is.

Silence

There are moments when we simply need to close our mouths and be silent.

For some, this is not easy. Practice. Practice some more.

When your mouth is silent, your other senses become more perceptive.

It is surprising how much more we *listen* when we give our mouth a rest. Hearing is not the same as listening. Hearing is the ability to perceive sound or receive noise. Listening is to hear with thoughtful attention, to be alert, to catch an expected sound. Sometimes God whispers like He did with Elijah in 1 Kings 19.

> A gentle, quiet voice entered into Elijah's ears.
> (*The Voice*)

Whispers are more easily heard when we simply stop speaking and just listen.

Stillness

Learning to practice the art of stillness is not always easy, but it is needed.

> Be still and know that I am God. (Psalm 46:10 NKJV)

Being still and allowing yourself to *rest* in God is *huge*. It allows us to clear away the clutter that sometimes hinders us from hearing His voice. It also boosts our individual creativity. Learning the art of stillness engages our ability to connect with God spirit-to-spirit! Yes, it is possible!

> There still remains a place of rest, a true Sabbath, for the people of God because those who enter into salvation's rest lay down their labors in the same way that God entered into a Sabbath rest from His. (Hebrews 4:8–9 *The Voice*)

As you try to create a space in your day to rest, guilt will probably rise up within you and remind you of all the "things" that are not being taken care. Ignore it, and just shift into trust. God is fully capable of holding your life together for you to rest! Rest refreshes you to be a better you! Resting in Him allows you to become a receiver of all that you need, and it unlocks your mind to operate on a whole new level of creativity.

As believers, we have the mind of Christ, so shouldn't we learn how to tap into our imagination and take it out for a spin. Who knows how many world-changing inventions and solutions are just waiting for us, to be still enough, for our minds to think of.

Praise

As we get to know the depth of God's unconditional love for us, His endless grace and His unswerving faithfulness in every detail of our lives, praising Him is a natural response! Praise is celebrating God with confidence! We can entrust ourselves fully to Him.

He is trustworthy; He is faithful; He is good. It is easy to focus our attention on God with our honor, praise, and adoration. Praise is rejoicing over His goodness and bragging over who He is.

> The Lord is my strength and my song, and He has become my salvation; He is my God, and I will praise Him; my father's God, and I will exalt Him. (Exodus 15:2 NKJV)

Praise is something we choose to do instead of basing it on what we are experiencing or feeling. While our situation and emotions may vary and change, God does not! He is constant, in a good mood, and He is the source of everything you need or hope for.

> I will sacrifice a freewill offering to You; I will praise Your name, O Lord, for it is good. (Psalm 54:6 NIV)

Here is a sample of what praise looks like:

> Praise that clings to who God is rather than to
> what we human beings see or do is a fundamental
> expression of faith. It is saying, I don't know
> what You are doing, why You are doing it, or
> how this whole thing is going to end up, but I
> trust You, God. I know You will be faithful to
> me. You will never abandon me. Therefore, I'm
> going to obey You in as much as I understand
> to do. The rest is up to You. I do this because
> You are my God and my Savior. All I have, am,
> and ever hope to be is Yours. Such praise frees
> God to work in our lives. (*The Power of Praise*,
> Myles Munroe)

There are many different forms of praise: speaking, singing, standing, kneeling, raising our hands, flagging, dancing. We are each unique and we get to express our heartfelt praise personally and creatively.

Worship

The only essential ingredient in worship is God's presence.

We are created for intimate communion with Him. As we yield ourselves to Him, He teaches us how to become a dwelling place for His presence.

> Therefore, let us all be thankful that we are a part of an unshakable Kingdom and offer to God worship that pleases Him and reflects the awe and reverence we have toward Him, for He is like a fierce fire that consumes everything. (Hebrews 12:28–29 *The Voice*)

Lose the concern you have to care more about what others may think of you, and wholeheartedly express your affection for Him. Sing your heart song to Him. Abandon yourself in worship.

Our one desire is to know Him.

CHAPTER 4

Your Mouth Is Enormously Potent

As we renew our mind in the truth that our words *create* reality, we begin to guard with keen awareness what we speak, what we declare, what we pray! Reminds me of a line in the movie *Spider-Man*: "With great power comes great responsibility."

Proverbs 18:21 (NKJV) tells us,

> Death and life are in the power of the tongue,
> and those who love it will eat its fruit.

I love the way *The Message* Bible breaks this verse down simply, stating,

> Words kill, words give life; they're either poison
> or fruit—you choose.

Controlling what comes out of our mouth is a great responsibility that each of us must individually bear. That should not intimidate us, but rather it should make us feel the weight of trust that God has placed in mankind, causing us to lean unto Him and partner with Him in all things as we use our mouths to let heaven invade earth.

How do we do that? Easy. It's all about *relationship*! As we spend time with God, we cultivate a history with Him. We get to know Him, ask Him questions, inquire of Him what to do in any given situation, and hear what He says and speak that!

Here are some avenues we can use to actively broker the reality of the kingdom of heaven here on earth right now.

Prayer/Intercession

For a long time, my devotional time with God looked like this: I would get up, go to a quiet place, read a passage from the Bible and maybe a page out of a daily devotional book, pray for what I thought would be great solutions to a number of issues and situations, thank Him, and then I was out the door . While my intentions were good and my prayers heartfelt, I did not have a relationship with Him. Relationship requires communication. While I was communicating to God, I did not give Him my time and attention to hear Him communicate to me.

As I began to give Him my attention, I found that His solutions were often very different from mine. Instead of praying out of an emotion or a reaction, I can go to God and, like many great warriors in the Bible, I get to inquire of the Lord. Then I listen and pray from a heart that is aligned with His heart.

Worship is essential in aligning our heart with His. Worship and prayer are so woven together that they simply cannot be separated! Praying out of a place or heart of worship allows us to actually pray arrows of answers, instead of praying what we think would be a good idea. We must cultivate an intimacy with Him that aligns our heart with His. How do we do that?

We learn to host His presence, to make ourselves an available landing strip for heaven to invade earth through us. That doesn't always mean soaking or praying for hours every day in our prayer closet—although there may be days that He summons us to do just that. Worship and prayer is simply being with Him as you go, living with your heart turned toward Him, abiding with Him, awake and expectant. As believers, we are all intercessors. It's not just something we do; it is who we are!

A key to a productive, joyful prayer life is worship If you have thirty minutes set aside to pray and intercede, worship for twenty-five of those minutes, and pray the remaining five. You can change the world in five minutes of praying His *heart*! As we cultivate a lifestyle of worship, we step into what Paul urges us to do in 1 Thessalonians 5:16–18,

> Rejoice always, pray without ceasing, in everything give thanks; for this is the will of God in Christ Jesus for you. (NKJV)

The only way we can do that is to stay in constant communion with Him. And yes, not only is that possible, it is what Jesus Himself prayed to the Father for us to experience!

> Holy Father, guard them as they pursue this life that you conferred as a gift through me, so they can be one heart and mind as we are one heart and mind. (John 17:11 *The Message*)

Partner in prayer with someone!

> When two of you get together on anything at
> all on earth and make a prayer of it, my Father
> in heaven goes into action. (Matthew 18–19 *The*
> *Message*)

Push past any feeling that would prevent you from doing this.
Find a friend, coworker, spouse, or family member; agree in
prayer, and you will see things happen.

Declarations

What you declare has enormous power. The Bible tells us in
Job 22:28,

> You will also declare a thing, And it will be
> established for you; So light will shine on your
> ways. (NKJV)

What we speak actually becomes a reality in our life. In other
words, our future will be positive or negative, depending on
what we choose to speak. Personal declarations from God's
Word helps produce a joyful, free future based on *truth*.

Speaking daily declarations, so that our own ears can hear
them, allows us to become deeply rooted in our identity in Him,

helps to develop our faith, and gives us the boldness to agree with and affirm the plans He has for our life.

Speaking daily declarations helps us renew our minds. You can create your own declarations by simply writing down verses that the Lord has quickened to you, which simply means that when you read them, something in your spirit is stirred up.

You can also Google "biblical declarations" and find many to read and choose from to help develop your own personal declarations. There are also books on this subject, one of my favorites being Steve and Wendy Backlund's book, *Igniting Faith in 40 Days*.

Here is a sample of my daily declarations. These declarations are taken from Scripture but have been personalized unless otherwise notated:

> This is the day the Lord has made, I will rejoice and be glad in it. (Psalm 118:24 NKJV)

> I can do all things through Christ who strengthens me. (Philippians 4:13 NKJV)

> God has not given me a spirit of fear, but of power and of love and of a sound mind. (2 Timothy 1:7)

Jesus Christ came that I might have life, and that I might have it more abundantly. (John 10:10)

I am redeemed and forgiven. (Ephesians 1:7)

Nothing can separate me from God"s love. (Romans 8:38)

I know the truth and the truth will set me free. (John 8:32)

I am lavished with His kindness and wisdom and understanding. (Ephesians 1:8)

God is for me. (Romans 8:31)

I am complete in Him, lacking nothing. (Colossians 2:10)

All my needs are supplied. (Philippians 4:19)

I am one spirit with the Lord. (1 Corinthians 6:17)

Greater is He who is in me than he who is in the world. (1 John 4:4)

I cast my care upon Him, for He cares for me. (1 Peter 5:7)

I have been blessed with every spiritual blessing. (Ephesians 1:3)

I seek first the Kingdom of God and His righteousness and all things will be added unto me. (Matthew 6:33)

My mouth establishes praise to silence the enemy. (Psalm 8:2)

My steps are ordered by The Lord. (Psalm 37:23)

I expect great things today. (1 Corinthians 2:9)

God said it. I believe it. That settles it. Amen.

Sometimes you may begin to declare a truth or promise from His Word that you know is true, but you don't yet fully believe it. No worries! As you keep declaring truth, He will establish it deep within you and enable you to believe.

Declarations can be kept on your phone or computer for you to read or meditate and for those times when speaking them out loud is not possible. If your declarations ever get joyless or routine, shift to some different ones for a while. Any Scripture that stirs your spirit can be turned into a prophetic declaration by personalizing it or setting it in present tense.

When we speak and declare His Word, we are choosing to believe and respond in faith to His words over the voice of our circumstance or any negative voice we may hear in our ears or in our minds.

Encouragement

Hope, support, and confidence can be given to those around us every day. It's free, easy, and potent. Take notice of an individual and ask God for something they need to hear or a thought that He thinks about them, and tell them. Everyone needs encouragement, friends, strangers, leaders, loved ones, and especially the individuals who live in your home with you. Family members who encourage each other and can call out the treasures in each other, even though they have different personalities and opposite ways of doing things, develop confidence in themselves, as well as the ability to celebrate the amazing things about others without the need to feel inferior or jealous. I am convinced that if everyone encouraged those around them, this act alone would change the world.

Testimony

Sharing with others what Jesus has done and is doing in our everyday life is vital. Hearing a testimony increases our faith and produces a boldness in us to step out of our comfort zone and pray for that person in the grocery store, give to someone in need, and to simply insert love whenever possible.

> For the testimony of Jesus is the spirit of prophecy. (Revelation 19:10 NKJV)

The definition of *prophecy* is a prediction of something to come. As we share and celebrate the testimonies of Jesus, we release the essence and power of heaven to see it happen again!

CHAPTER 5

Knowing Who You Are

You are unconditionally loved by Papa God. No matter what you do, or do not do, His love for you never changes.

When you say yes to Jesus and choose to make Him Lord of your life, you are reconnecting into the family of God and are now a son or a daughter of the King. This will require a new way of thinking. As we get to know Him, we have to shift our minds from what we think about ourselves to what He thinks about us. God so lovingly helps us do that by showering us with His love, washing away all the lies that we believe, and allowing us to see ourselves as He does—accepted and in right standing with Him.

Saying yes to Jesus does not magically erase some of the inner issues that have been formed from our past. We all have wounds; we all have people we need to forgive, and we all sometimes get stuck in this process of renewing our mind to His way of thinking. One thing that was key in helping me get free of the baggage in my mind was Sozo Ministry (what also is called Breakthrough or Prayer Ministry). This is simply a process of one being able to open up and share the deep things about him or herself in a safe environment, and be ministered to by a team of trustworthy believers who partner with Holy Spirit in helping us become free and whole.

Many times in the Bible when the word *salvation* (*sozo*) is written, it actually means saved, healed, and delivered. I found the best explanation of the word *sozo* in the training manual *Basic Sozo* by Dawna DeSilva and Teresa Liebscher. It states,

> ""Sozo," which is used 110 times in the New Testament, is a Greek word meaning, "to save or make well or whole." According to the <u>Strong's Greek Dictionary of the New Testament</u>, "Sozo" also means, "to save, deliver, heal and preserve." The writers of the New Testament showed the completeness of the word "Sozo" by using it in different contexts to refer to each aspect of salvation.
>
> Here are a few examples of these New Testament verses that describe the three aspects of "Sozo": salvation, healing, and deliverance.

SALVATION:

> That if you confess with your mouth Jesus is Lord and believe in your heart that God raised Him raised Him from the dead you shall be <u>saved</u> [Sozo].
>
> Romans 10:9

> For the Son of Man came to seek and to <u>save</u> [Sozo] what was lost.
>
> Luke 19:10

HEALING:

> But Jesus turning and seeing her said, "Daughter, take courage, your faith has made you <u>well</u>" [Sozo], and at once the woman was made <u>well</u> [Sozo].
>
> Matthew 9:22

DELIVERANCE:

> And those who had seen it reported to them how the man who was demon-possessed had been made well [<u>Sozo</u>].
>
> Luke 8:36"

We often stop at just salvation and never experience the healing and deliverance. God meant for us to receive all three, which means He wants us to be whole. Getting free of the things in our past so that we can step into the destiny God has designed for each of us is essential, in order to be victorious. We need to be whole in body, soul, and spirit. In this process of being ministered to we learn some essential tools that teach us how to keep ourselves free after we leave the ministry session.

I believe everyone can benefit from this ministry. We all have inner issues that, if not dealt with, can keep us locked up from our true identity in Him. I have had several ministry sessions and now make a point to have a session at least once a year.

This *sozo* or Breakthrough Ministry is not just for adults; my own children, who have not been abused or neglected, have wounds and issues on their hearts that need to be dealt with and healed. Some of those issues may have even been caused by me, even though I would have never done that intentionally. As a parent, I want them free and whole, and I love them way more than I care what they might need to discuss about me in a ministry session. In fact, it will only serve to make our relationship stronger. Wholeness is, after all, an ongoing and intentional process.

When we are cut free from the baggage of our past, we can freely step into who we truly are, and that is unconditionally loved, extremely valued, and totally amazing! Yes, you are! I love the way Graham Cooke puts it: "If Jesus is in you and one of His names is wonderful … then that makes you at least potentially astonishing."

If you don't see yourself as *amazing*, those of us around you will only see a glimpse of who you really are. We will just see "ama" without getting to view the *zing*! The world needs your *zing*, your unique flavor. We need for you to be everything He has designed you to be!

If seeing yourself as totally amazing seems hard for you, spend time with God, meditate on who He is, and let His love and delight settle over you until this truth resonates deep within you.

Loving yourself is vital because His Word instructs us to love others as we do ourselves. I cannot give to others what I do not have. When I receive His love for me and align my thinking with His, I am then able to love others out of that same radical love. The more time I spend with Him, the more I am changed by His great love and the more my heart expands and is enlarged in its capacity to genuinely love those around me.

The individuals around you every day are amazing! Now I know that's easy for us to say about some people, but it is actually true about even that difficult one you may be thinking about and shaking your head over. Amazing is in there. You just need to look past some things to see it and call out the true treasure of who they are from God's point of view.

We often work alongside someone and never really engage with them or know them. The world often influences us to strive to become independent, but we were created and designed for fellowship and covenant! We need each other, and love is the key.

We must understand God has an individual destiny for each of us, and if we encourage, celebrate, and help others succeed in their destiny, it doesn't take us away from our destiny or short change us in any way. When we know that God is capable and confident in His specific plans for each of us, it becomes very easy to encourage others and invest in them, to fulfill even the biggest of dreams.

Picture yourself looking through a telescope into His realm, seeing the "end" game and realizing that only those things that matter there are really the only things that matter here. On the other side of eternity, the things that seem to be so important to us here and now won't even make the crossing. What will matter most is: Did you love? Did you take the time to help, celebrate, fellowship with and be there for others, even when you didn't agree with them, even when you saw how different we are? Did you choose to look past everything that will not matter in eternity and simply, genuinely love them on purpose?

Personally, applying this eternal view is helping me to dismiss thoughts and actions that would hinder me from loving another, regardless of what they say or do. I want them to be on the other side of eternity alongside me as one body—a bride joined with Christ.

I am amazing because He is amazing. I am a woman who has tasted of the love and goodness of God, and I am learning who He is and what He is like. His love and goodness is transforming me into looking and becoming just like Him! He is not intimidated by my faults or my shortcomings; He gives me mercies anew every day, and He chooses to forget on purpose the negative things in my past—loves me as I am, calls me into the name He has spoken over me, and celebrates who He knows I am becoming.

Applying this eternal focus allows me to do the same with others, following His example, of forgetting the negative, loving others as they are, calling others into greatness, and celebrating who He knows they are.

You are amazing, the people around you are amazing, and we need all the creative potential that God has placed in each of us to fully cover the earth with His glory!

CHAPTER 6

A Blank Canvas

One day as I was sitting in a swing—reading, resting, pondering—and just being with Him when I had this thought come into my mind: *Blank canvas*. I knew this thought was too random and too specific to be just something that popped into my head. This was the Lord speaking. So I asked Him, "What is that? What does blank canvas mean?"

Into my thoughts came these questions: *Can you live each day as a blank canvas? Can you wake up each day with Me and choose to purposely leave yesterday out of today? Leave any negative or hurtful thing that has happened. Leave regret over what did not happen. Leave even that amazing, beautiful thing that you got to experience. Can you leave it in yesterday and just become a blank canvas for this day? Can you stop worrying about the future, not be anxious over what might or might not come? Can you not put off for another day what should be for this today? Can you come to Me as a blank canvas, not dragging anything into today from yesterday and not pulling anything from tomorrow into today, just come as you are and be with Me? Become the paintbrush. Lean unto me, and give yourself to my hand and let Me dip you into the colors I have planned and designed for this day alone. Let's create a work of art that is today!*

> Give your entire attention to what God is doing right now and don't get worked up about what may or may not happen tomorrow. (Matthew 6:34 *The Message*)

I knew this was more than just a suggestion; I knew that if I could honestly do that, it would change my life. I simply said, "Yes, help me become a blank canvas each day." That verse about the mercies of God being new every morning came to mind—Lamentations 3:22–23.

I began to ponder what this would look like for me. My pursuit to walk out this blank-canvas life looked like this: "God, I want to worship you fresh and vibrantly each day. I desire to know you in a new way today. Yesterday was quite amazing; but today is a new day, and I hunger to experience your love and presence as though I have never known you—as though I only have *this* day."

I will admit, leaving regret in the past was a tough one for me. Nothing to do but forgive myself and let it go, *lay it down*. Discovering the freedom of not being overly concerned with tomorrow, I began to fully place my trust in Him! Kind of like being on a roller coaster you could potentially die on, you have a choice: you can grip the bar so tight that you pull a muscle, or you can trust it, lift your hands to the sky, and become one with the ride!

I began doing this each day with Him and experiencing the most glorious freedom. Words to describe it: easy, fluid, peaceful, joyful, natural—like I had stepped into the rhythm of Eden as Adam and Eve must have experienced in the beginning.

As I am still learning to get my bearings in this Eden rhythm, I hear God ask, *"Can you let others come to you as a blank canvas too? Can you leave in yesterday anything negative that has happened, hurts, disappointments, or wounds? Can you give them mercies new every day like I give you? Can you love them as if you have never met them and as though you will never get another day with them to celebrate who they are, encourage them, breath in their unique flavor, and smear them with love?"* My response was the same, "Yes, help me do that."

Walking out this revelation is deepening my relationship with God and with others. This doesn't mean that I don't think ahead or make plans for tomorrow; I just don't let the things designed for tomorrow change my today. Nor does it mean that I forget my history with God; I just refuse to let how I knew Him yesterday determine how I get to know Him today. This has caused me to fall more in love with Jesus, more in love with God, more in love with the Holy Spirit. This enables me to love myself more, which allows me to freely and genuinely love others and they get to be around me with a clean, fresh slate each new day!

Practicing this blank canvas as a lifestyle has caused a creative explosion within me! My thoughts are more precise; I am happy all over; I am excited about the possibilities God has placed in myself and in others; and I am partnering with Holy Spirit to call them out!

We can hang out on the threshold of salvation near death, waiting for His return, or we can walk boldly through the doorway that is Jesus and into experiencing the kingdom of heaven on earth. A victorious reality where God's love overwhelms us expands our capacity to actually love others as ourselves and allows us to demonstrate His power on earth through intimacy with Him.

CHAPTER 7

In Process

The other day I felt like God made this statement to me, "I will give you the desires of your heart ... even if they are not My first choice."

Yeah, go back and read that again, and give it a minute to settle in.

We want His desires, His plans to unfold through our lives, and we can ... but I believe it is more up to us than we realize. God is God. He is sovereign, and yet I can cap off His plans for me because He, in His great love, chooses to honor my free will. That causes me to tremble, not out of fear of Him but of me stopping short of all He designed me for, which would mean me giving Him less than the whole of me. Co-union with Him is His desire, not a robotic family who is programmed or shows up out of duty or obligation. We were made to love!

We are in a process—a friend reminded me this week that she is not the same as she was six months ago, or a year ago, or three years ago. We are in a process of becoming like Him. Celebrate that! Look at where He has brought you and rejoice! You can love at a deeper level than you once could!

Yay God! Look back on your journey with the Lord; look where He has been with you: meeting you at your level of need, placing that person in your life at just the right time, leading you to that book that was the key to break through, freedom experienced in prayer ministry, songs that allowed you to sing the cry of your heart, CD teachings, conferences, learning His Word with the

Holy Spirit, being in the secret place with Him … You are not the same as you were! Rejoice!

> And I am convinced *and* sure of this very thing, that He Who began a good work in you will continue until the day of Jesus Christ—right up to the time of His return—developing [that good work] *and* perfecting *and* bringing it to full completion in you. (Philippians 1:6 AB)

If you are wondering what the end result of seeking Him first looks like, I can tell you. It looks like love. Whatever you enjoy or feel called to do—firefighter, stay-at-home mom, musician, business person, teacher—what God is doing *in* you as you enjoy getting to know Him is preparing you to love, through whatever you do. He's in us, and no doubt we are amazing; but without love, we are just a clanging sound that is of no lasting effect!

If I were to go mountain climbing with a group of explorers and after climbing for a week in the snow and ice in frigid conditions we reached base camp, I can choose to remain there while they continue the journey. On our spiritual journeys we have base camps too! Often it is not easy to keep climbing. God loves us no less if we choose to remain where we are … but He so encourages us to run the race because His love for us woos us into the very thing that completes us and satisfies us … and that is Him. That is *love*. Jesus gave all for us. He deserves nothing less in return!

When we find the climb hard, we must remember that we have the most experienced guide ever, the Holy Spirit, right there beside us. If we reach an impasse along the way, *stop* and *inquire* of Him, He will know what to do! In your quest to reach the top of the mountain, know that the goal at the top is not your ministry, your purpose or His will ... that is something you develop with Him along the journey. At the top is Him. He is *love*.

The more I seek Him, the more I find Him; the more I take time to be loved on by Him, the more loving I become. Being with Him changes ME. It changes how I see, how I hear, how I love. Spending time with Him changes how I intercede. Yes, this is a personal quest--but it is also a "bridal" one! Like the quote from the movie *BackDraft*, "Where we go one, we go all." If we contend united in prayer, we will see things shift. If we do not, we won't. Simple truth. We have much more control over what goes on in this world than we think. He did, after all, give us authority on the earth!

> The heaven, *even* the heavens, *are* the LORD's;
> But the earth He has given to the children of
> men. (Psalm 115:16 NKJV)

I believe as we cultivate intimacy with Him and each other, climbing this mountain together, we will begin to see power released through us because of His established love within us.

> For the kingdom of God is not in word but in
> power. (1 Corinthians 4:20 NKJV)

We are all designed to walk in power, but why would He give me power if I am not rooted in love? I would be dangerous, destructive, and, in my quest to reach the top of the mountain, my goal would be the power and not Him.

"I will give you the desires of your heart ... even if they are not my first choice" ... let's not stop short of climbing into the all that God has designed for each of us and let's take the time to aide and assist those around us and actually climb together! The quote "Where we go one we go all" sounds like the kingdom of heaven invading earth via a love encounter with Jesus.

Dust off the desires of your heart and share them with others. Let us hear about the dreams within each other. Shake off the disappointments of the past, and let the wind of heaven blow away those instances when someone shot holes in your dreams! Let us refuse to cap off the plans that God has designed for each of us. Let us refuse to let those around us cap off the plan that God has designed specifically for them.

A friend of mine shared something so profound after he and a group from our church returned from a mission trip. He spoke to us about what had most impacted him on the trip, specifically about how going to a foreign country made him aware of how important and valuable it was to spend time with others.

We can say and do a great deal of wonderfully good things, but at the end of the day, if those we come into contact with don't experience love, what's the point. Often we do things that seem loving to us, but in reality are not felt as love to the one in front of us.

If the one in front of us is going to feel loved, it simply requires time. I believe that time is the most valuable thing we have to give because wrapped inside of it is love, which leads us back to looking like Him. We get to enjoy the process of becoming like Him as we lean into the woo of knowing Him.

CHAPTER 8

Living Victorious

God's Word tells us that the Enemy comes to kill, steal, and destroy, but Jesus came so that we could have life and have it abundantly! God simply trumps the Enemy—always.

Do not be surprised by the Enemy's attempts to bombard us with what I call Enemy "fodder" as we continue to mature, renew our minds, and fall deeper in love with God! As we worship, we are actually pressing into more intimacy with Abba and intentionally seeking more of the kingdom of heaven on earth in our everyday lives. The Enemy will always try to distract us with anything that will stop us from that, from more intimacy, more freedom, more truth, more Abba! But let us remember that Jesus kicked his butt. And in Matthew 16:18b–19 NKJV, he tells us,

> I will build my church and the gates of hell shall not prevail against it. I will give you the keys of the kingdom of heaven, and whatever you bind on earth shall be bound in heaven, and whatever you loose on earth shall be loosed in heaven.

Above the Snake Line

As we learn to apply the truths, we learn and intentionally occupy the promises of God we get to live above the "snake line." For those of you who have never heard of this, the snake line is a particular plateau above sea level where snakes cannot live.

In a spiritual context, part of living above the snake line means living from a place of such utter safety that we live out of the reach of the Enemy. It is only through our oneness and completeness in Him that we gain the capacity and the confidence to actually live this way.

As we cultivate a secret life with God, we find that He hides us and safely shelters us, but look where He hides us! It's not tucked away out of sight; He hides us high up on a rock, safe above the snake line right and out in the open for all to see. He puts us there and presents us as a light to the world.

> His house is my shelter and secret retreat. *It is there I find peace* in the midst of storm and turmoil. Safety sits with me in the hiding place of God. He will set me on a rock, *high above the fray.* (Psalm 27:5 *The Voice*)

We operate from a place of victory! We have been given many tools to use in spiritual warfare. Laughter is a massive weapon to wield at the enemy. The fruits of the spirit (love, joy, peace, patience, kindness, goodness, faithfulness, gentleness, self-control) are also crushing weapons of warfare. Abiding in rest and allowing our focus to remain on Jesus is priority, so ask for wisdom; pull out whatever you need, and use it! Let nothing prevent you from pressing into deeper intimacy with God.

Taking Ownership

Becoming enmeshed with God will cost you! Stepping into communion with Him requires taking ownership and responsibility of your own spiritual condition and growth. As we give Him the best of who we are and we are willing to sacrifice what is most precious to us, for Him, we step into our inheritance as sons and daughters.

In the book of Genesis, we read that Moses intentionally *turned aside* to see the bush that was on fire but not being consumed. That is how we must be about dating God—intentional about pursuing and growing in intimacy with Him. You can attend church on Sunday, listen to and apply what your pastor has to say, but if that is the only time during the week that you are feeding your spirit then you are spiritually starving.

God places pastors, spiritual leaders, teachers, mentors, and others around us to nurture and aide us as we grow in relationship with Him, but the weight of that job is not on their shoulders, it is on ours. Each of us determines the level of intimacy we get to enjoy with God.

That's actually a good thing, because it also means that no one can limit or cap off what I get to experience with God; that is on me. No one can limit or cap off what you get to experience with God; that is on you. We determined that by choice.

God has graciously allowed me to be pastored by some amazing men and women; and every one of them has poured into my life beautifully, but they are not perfect. Every one of them has made a mistake. So what?

As we read in the Bible about David, we discover that he made some massive mistakes; yet, David's heart was turned toward God. He lived in an intentional awareness of communion with God. His heart condition was toward God and enmeshed with God to such an extent that God called him a man after his own heart! That is a beautiful example to reach out and grab hold of.

I love my pastors and their spouses, and part of loving them is not holding them to a standard of perfection, which would just be setting all of us up for failure because it is an unreasonable expectation. In fact, when someone in leadership is brave enough to share a personal mistake and allow God to use it as a display of his redemptive grace and love, it pierces into the inner core of my heart and allows me to see and experience God in a new way.

Our spiritual growth and maturity in God is certainly enhanced by other individuals, circumstances, resources, nature, movies, etc. In fact, when we live with our heart turned toward God, He can, and will, use anything He chooses to reveal His love and nature to us.

He chose us, and we get to say yes to Him, by choice, every day.

In the game of football, it is essential to have the ball in order to score. Living a victorious life will also require us to have the ball and operate from an offensive position. A helpful way to spiritually keep the ball is to increase the time you spend praying in the Spirit. This may be the most powerful thing we do on any given day.

> But you, dear friends, carefully build yourselves up in this most holy faith by praying in the Holy Spirit, staying right at the center of God's love, keeping your arms outstretched, ready for the mercy of our Master, Jesus Christ. (Jude 1:20 *The Message*)

I encourage you to pray in tongues, sing in the Spirit, praise Him in your own unique expression in every moment possible. Make it a habit to do this as often as you can—as you shower, get dressed, cook, drive—just make it a part of your everyday life, and watch what happens.

There is nothing that can separate you from God and His unconditional love. This revelation allows us to band together in community, loving one another and pressing into intimacy with Him … knowing that we are victorious and that the God of the universe is our rear guard. Take the fodder that the Enemy throws toward, you and convert it into a fuel that ignites your passion and causes you to take a swan dive into the very heart of God. We are not operating from a defensive position so take the ball and "bust a move" to bring the kingdom of heaven to Earth.

Victorious living requires developing the discipline of keeping our focus on Jesus. I have heard that it only takes about ten minutes for our focus to drift, which means that we get to purposely choose Him every ten minutes as we turn our affection back to Him. Carol Arnott shares a great tool for helping form a habit of keeping our focus on Jesus, and that is to have a ten-minute timer. You can purchase a timer that clips on your clothes; or you can download the app Worship10m on your phone, and every ten minutes it will vibrate. The results of constantly focusing on Jesus with thanksgiving and praise are amazing: spiritually, physically, and emotionally.

As we learn to keep our focus and gaze on Him, He gives us wisdom and instruction in what to do in any situation, whether it is to simply ignore the Enemy completely or rise up and take authority over him.

I am reminded of a story that I heard about a man who was being harassed by the Enemy. The man took an empty chair and told the Enemy to sit in it and watch him worship God!

We need to ask Holy Spirit for wisdom because there are times when we need to be gentle like a lamb, and then there are times when we need to let the lion in us *roar*!

CHAPTER 9

Dating God

If we so choose, we get to daily experience an ongoing, mind-altering, off-the-chart, personal revival.

> To Him who by His power that is at work within us can do surpassingly more than all we ask or imagine. (Ephesians 3:20 *Williams Translation*)

> Now to Him Who, by (in consequence of) the [action of His] power that is at work within us, is able to [carry out His purpose and] do superabundantly, far over *and* above all that we [dare] ask or think—infinitely beyond our highest prayers, desires, thoughts, hopes or dreams. (Ephesians 3:20 AB)

How does one unlock the reality of that Scripture? We intentionally engage in pursuing a relationship with the very one who created us specifically to enjoy relationship with. We date God!

That may mess up your theology a bit; it did mine the first time I heard it! I was discussing with one of my college-aged children the importance and pleasure of knowing and interacting with Holy Spirit; we began to talk about what that actually looks like on a daily basis and as we did out of my mouth came the words, "You should just date God!" Hearing that surprised us both, but I totally knew that God had slipped those words out of my mouth because I would not have come up with that on my own! God is sneaky and will sometimes hide His voice in the mouth of a friend, a stranger, or, like in that case, within the words from our own lips.

As I thought about what I had said, I realized the magnitude of truth within them; after all, we are the bride of Christ! It makes perfect sense that we would choose to cultivate a personal, ongoing relationship with the one we have said yes to share all of eternity with.

Dating God looks like enjoying Jesus on a daily basis, experiencing an active relationship with Holy Spirit, learning the nature of Father God—the many ways that He speaks, His promises, His ways, what He likes, what He laughs over or celebrates, as well as what He dislikes and the things that cause His heart to hurt. It means being one with Him and allowing your heart to be calibrated to the rhythm of His.

> Stay focused on what's above, not on earthly things, because your old life is dead and gone. Your new life is now hidden, enmeshed with the Anointed who is in God. (Colossians 3:3 *The Voice*)

The word *enmesh* is a beautiful word! This word is usually used in the context of describing something negative because it means to be wrapped up or tangled in someone or something. To me, enmesh describes and creates a visual picture of what happens when we actively and intentionally date God. We become tangled in his nature, rooted in His ways, and wrapped up in His goodness and love.

> You must be deeply rooted, your foundations must be strong enough to grasp the idea of the breadth and length, the height and depth, yes to come at last to know the love of Christ, although it far surpasses human understanding, so that you may be filled with the perfect fullness of God. (Ephesians 3:17–19 *Williams Translation*)

God enjoys your presence! As you purposely enmesh yourself in fellowship and communion with God, you experience a completeness deep within that cannot be attained through any other means. He simply completes us.

The more time I spend with Him and the more I allow myself to become enmeshed in Him, He exponentially enlarges my capacity to be like Him. As a result of that, I may get to see and do amazing things that are birthed out of my intimacy with the Creator of all things, but it is in the abiding with Him that I find complete fullness.

If your mind is still reeling from the concept of dating God, keep in mind that yes, God is the omniscient One, He's omnipresent, He is the I AM, and He is genuinely, compassionately, and actively concerned about every single thing in our life. He cares about even the smallest details and does so with a heart of unbridled, unconditional love. He is our cheerleader, our biggest fan, our intercessor; He is our father, our mother, our sister, and our brother. He is our source, our guide, and the one we can put our complete confidence and trust in. He is the only one who is actually capable of backing up everything He says! As I lean unto trusting Him and entangle myself in Him, I experience Him in new, ongoing ways as His world and realm invade mine.

One day, while hanging out with God, He said, "I'm just God, standing in front of you, asking to love you." I melted with love for Him! Anyone familiar with the movie *Notting Hill* remembers the line that Julia Roberts says to Hugh Grant: "I'm just a girl, standing in front of a boy, asking him to love her." God knew that line would affect me; He simply altered the words to reveal His heart to me! Yes, He is brilliant. He speaks in a manner of how He knows we listen.

CHAPTER 10

It's All about Love!

At the end of the day, did we love? Love is actually all around us; we just have to engage in it actively and intentionally, which is part of enmeshment.

That simply looks like me stepping out, opening up my heart to those around me, and getting to know the flavor of whom they are! In the process of letting him love us, we learn how to love others on a deeper level.

For example, my husband, whom I love beyond words, greatly benefits from the fact that I love God more than I love him because as I grow in fellowship with God, He allows me to see fresh aspects of his uniqueness that I have never noticed in the many years we have been married. God shows me things about him that causes me to say, "Wow, look at that! I've never seen that before!" As a result I get to fall in love with my husband on a deeper level, over and over again.

That same thing is happening with people in general; the more I hang out with God, the more that I see in and about others to love! Often, I am a little bit blown away by the unique creative expression of each individual, and my heart is enlarged with compassion to serve him or her well. I find delight in loving others as I love myself.

And, I'm only at the beginning of knowing how to love. I know this because one day out of the blue God said to me, "I'm only at the beginning of loving you." As I pondered that, I realized that

God's love for me doesn't change, but my capacity to receive the magnitude of His love does. My capacity to be loved increases as I spend time in His presence, which increases my capacity to love.

Authentic Fellowship

This kind of fellowship goes beyond the surface interactions that we often experience with most individuals as we go about each day. Authentic fellowship is being willing to tear off a piece of oneself and share it with another and receiving a piece from them. This fellowship requires risk and trust. Allowing ourselves to be real and open with each other is biblical, and in doing so it totally cuts the legs out from under anything that the enemy could possibly use to trip us up.

I need to be surrounded by individuals who are maturing in Christ who help me to grow, answer questions, encourage and correct me, pray with me, and help become established in my identity in Christ.

> Let the message of Christ continue to live in you
> in all its wealth of wisdom; keep on teaching it
> to one another and training one another in it
> with thankfulness, in your hearts singing praise
> to God with psalms, hymns, and spiritual songs.
> (Colossians 3:16 *Williams Translation*)

Jesus modeled this for us with the twelve disciples. He spent three years teaching them about the kingdom and the nature of God. They were as one family and they experienced all of the interesting attributes of each other's personality, talents, passions, and quirks as well as their shortcomings, mistakes, and failures. God himself created us and designed us to be part of a family, a family that communes together in unity.

Unity is not conformity. Sometimes we make the mistake of wanting everyone to be just like us because we have an idea that is what unity is supposed to look like, but nothing could be further from the truth. Unity is having all different kinds of flavors coming together in love, honoring one another, and molding together as one unit. That is what covenant is all about … knowing that I have a weakness in a specific area that you have a strength in and that I have a strength in a specific area that you have a weakness in, we can partner together in covenant so that what is mine becomes yours and what is yours becomes mine. This way we actually get to celebrate each other without limits or jealousy because we are one body moving to gather with God as our Father.

> Since you are all set apart by God, made holy and
> dearly loved, clothe yourselves with *a holy way of*
> *life:* compassion, kindness, humility, gentleness,
> and patience. Put up with one another. Forgive.
> Pardon any offenses against one another, as the
> Lord has pardoned you, because you should act

in kind. But above all these, put on love! Love is
the perfect tie to bind these together. (Colossians
3:12–14 *The Voice*)

Experiencing authentic fellowship with one another is a vital
part of learning and knowing what God is like. Even though
you may not be in your pastor's inner circle of friends, or
your teacher's or someone in leadership, no worries; God will
surround you with an inner circle of specific individuals with
whom you can share the deep intimacies of your heart.

Authentic relationship is founded in truth and requires a
willingness to communicate, share, and listen, even when it
may not be easy or convenient. Intimacy in any relationship
requires the risk of opening up your heart and allowing them
to see inside. In his DVD series "Keep Your Love On," Danny
Silk breaks down the word intimacy so beautifully:

intimacy—"into-me-see"

With God this is easy, because He already knows everything
about you and loves you with an everlasting, joyful, and
unconditional love. As we receive His love and wholeness we
gain confidence and boldness in developing authentic fellowship
with others.

So I give you a new command: Love each other
deeply and fully. Remember the ways that I have

loved you, and demonstrate your love for others
in those same ways. (John 13:34 *The Voice*)

Flavors of His Nature

I understand that some individuals are easier to love than others.
That was once a problem for me because there were some people
that I just did not like, and God decided to let me in on how
He felt about those particular individuals. He reminded me of
when I was younger and my parents would take me to Baskin-
Robbins. I would look at all the many, many colorful flavors
that were before me, and I would always choose chocolate. God
asked me why I always chose chocolate, and I responded that it
was the flavor I liked! He said, "I like them all."

That began to change how I saw and interacted with people
I encountered every day. I began to specifically look for the
uniqueness that set them apart from others, and I would ask
God to help me to see people as He does, so that I could enjoy
their flavor too. If we look closely and allow Holy Spirit to help,
we get to see an aspect of God's nature in each person. After
all, we are created in His image, and God is so big that it would
take all of us being uniquely who He created us to be to even
begin to give us a snapshot into the vastness of what He is like.

So now I enjoy people and their unique flavor, choosing often to
look past what I see with my own eyes and let Him show me the

view through His. What I am discovering is that every person has amazing within them; they are creative, they have gifts, they have something the world needs, and we get to partner with God in helping to release the treasures within them! Again, it all goes back to relationship and relationship begins with love.

Living as One

What if we got up each day and as we went about our daily tasks we were to embrace other people as though they were family? For example, if you're at the grocery store and someone in front of you is having a bad day, treat them as though they were a member of your family. If we did, we would take a moment and try to help them by looking past their actions, help discover what they are in need of, and help to meet that need.

If the finger on my right hand is injured, I don't ignore it. I address the issue and take care of the wound because I need this finger, and I don't want to live in pain. Why not expand that same desire to care for the body of Christ and apply it on a global scale by each of us being intentional about loving the person in front of us?

What if we did this with all people, as we went about our day, whether we knew them or not, choosing to live awakened to the necessity of caring for each other? Imagine that, living as though we are all connected, individual parts of one great big family.

> All the glory You have given to Me, I pass on to
> them. May that glory unify them and make them
> one as We are one, I in them and You in Me, that
> they may be refined so that all will know that
> You sent Me, and You love them in the same way
> You love Me. (John 17:22–23 *The Voice*)

Remember, we are ambassadors of Christ, each of us, a
walking embassy fully able to meet the need of another person
by releasing the kingdom of God. That is what Jesus did; He
changed the world by being intentional and compassionate
about addressing any issue that kept a person from experiencing
freedom. He spent time with His Father; He knew who He was;
and He lovingly brokered what was needed to those around
Him. And then He prayed that we would experience the same.

We Are Ambassadors

An ambassador is someone who is from another place and
represents the government of the territory they are from. When
we surrender our heart to Jesus and make Him Lord of our life,
we become ambassadors of Christ and citizens of the kingdom
of heaven. As ambassadors we get to represent the government
of heaven here on earth. How do we do that? We have become
His dwelling place, so wherever we go, we take the kingdom
of heaven with us. In other words, you are a walking embassy
brokering heaven in your own sphere of influence.

When the Roman Empire was conquering new territories they did not bring those that they conquered back to Rome. They simply set up the newly conquered territory to look just like Rome. That is what we are to do, take over territory for the kingdom of God, as an ambassador of Christ, representing the kingdom of God as we go about our daily life. We simply become like yeast and allow the love and goodness of God to be stirred into the people we encounter each day by practicing the character of our King, Jesus.

Bill Johnson describes it this way, "They will be drawn to your light, as sons and daughters of God, others will see how amended we are from our brokenness and come to receive their answer. We connect them to the Lord. We are a revived people restored back to communion with God, filled with Jesus, being guided in all things by Holy Spirit who in essence gives us the blueprint of how to do life. Then we are sprinkled into the lives of others like yeast so that they can experience it too."

As ambassadors of Christ we get to love people right where they are. I don't have to force others into doing what I feel is right or what may be right for me. I get to represent what God is like, expose others to Him and allow them to encounter His perfect love. His love will begin to woo their affection toward Him and just like Moses they will turn aside, wanting to know more!

He is so good that you cannot keep Him to yourself! His love and goodness begins to fill you to the point that you overflow and leak Him onto others. As we begin to step into our true identity in Him, we begin to love and naturally minister to others. I believe that is how the glory of the Lord is going to cover the earth as the water covers the sea.

> For the earth will be filled With the knowledge of the glory of the Lord, As the waters cover the sea. (Habakkuk 2:14 NKJV)

There is no part of the sea that is not water, so God intends for the whole entire Earth to be covered with His glory. You get to be you. God will take you and reveal the treasures that He has hidden specifically and uniquely within you and present you as a gift to the world. He knows the very thing that you enjoy the most, even if you are not yet aware of what that is; and He sets you up to love others and minister out of the very thing that gives you the most joy. You get to point others to Jesus whether you are a student, mechanic, lawyer, waitress, chef, doctor, a mom who homeschools, or a ramp agent at an airport. You get to be a nexus for others to receive what they need. Genuinely loving others creates a landing strip for His presence and in His presence everything is possible.

We were created to be loved and to love. Yet sometimes we fight against that very thing, and when we do, we limit ourselves to only a measure of the life He has designed for us. But when we lean into His woo and become one with Him we begin to experience the fullness of life as He designed it.

BREAD CRUMBS

(Resources)

We grow out of childhood, but we are to always remain childlike, living each day with expectancy, wonder, and being intentionally teachable.

As a child of God, a parent, a wife, a friend, I am always open to tools that help me develop relationships and that aid me in developing intimacy with Papa God. What I learn, I pass on to others. Often these tools come in the form of books, CDs, podcasts, etc.; what took someone years to learn in their own personal walk with God, I get to receive, apply, and walk in—all in the amount of time it takes me to read their book or listen to their teaching and absorb the revelation! I get to pass that revelation along to my children and others so that they get to enjoy God on a deeper level, right now, enabling them to encounter even greater experiences and revelation with Him!

The Internet has enabled me to be taught and mentored by many individuals that I don't personally know. If you happen to enjoy the Internet as a result of God's great gift of love to me. You are welcome. Enjoy!

And yes, I know that all sites and all social media are not good. That's why we need to ask for wisdom and learn the art of self-management. If we are honest, sometimes we need a little less Facebook and a lot more of His face and His book. Holy Spirit helps us with finding a healthy balance. He is brilliant and always happy to help.

Below are some of the mentors and resources that God gave me that helped me cultivate a relationship with Him and continue to do so. In addition to reading the books listed, I also enjoy listening and watching their messages as well! I have included their current websites, as many of my mentors have CDs, DVDs, mp3 and mp4 downloads, and many other resources that are easily available that may enhance your journey to know Him.

Remember you are unique so your journey will be as well. My bread crumbs may not be the bread crumbs God uses to woo you. My hope is that they will be for you like a set of starting blocks used when running track: a solid base from which to launch.

So here you go! I leave you with some of the precious men and women in the body of Christ that God chose to use in wooing me through the door of salvation into knowing Him and His love!

Myles Munroe: *Rediscovering the Kingdom, Understanding the Purpose and Power of Prayer, Purpose and Power of Praise*
mylesmunroeinternational.com

Bill Johnson: *The Supernatural Power of the Transformed Mind, When Heaven Invades Earth, Face to Face with God, Strengthening Yourself in the Lord: How to Release the Hidden Power of God in Your Life, Hosting the Presence: Unveiling Heaven's Agenda, Supernatural Ways of Royalty: Discovering Your Rights and Privileges of Being a Son or Daughter of God* (with Kris Vallotton), *Essential Guide to Healing* (with Randy Clark).

CDs: *It Is Finished, Your History with God, The Supernatural Power of the Transformed Mind, What It Means to Be Forgiven, Hosting the Presence, Friendship With God, The Power of the Testimony, Intentional Parenting: Kingdom Perspectives on Raising Revivalists, Grace? ... Hell Yes, Faith Anchored in the Unseen, The Healing Collection, The Transformation Collection.* ibethel.org and bethel.tv

Graham Cooke: *Beholding and Becoming, Hiddenness and Manifestation, Crafted Prayer, The Nature of God, The Language of Promise, Towards a Powerful Inner Life, Living in Dependency and Wonder, God's Keeping Power,* (these eight small books can be purchased as a set), *Secret Sayings Hidden Meanings, Radical Perceptions, Keys to Brilliant Focus* (The Wisdom Series), *Permission Granted.*

CDs: *The Graham Cooke Compendium* Vol. 1, *The Art Of Thinking Brilliantly, The Practice of Delight.* brilliantbookhouse.com

Beni Johnson: *The Happy Intercessor* (book/DVD), *Prayer Servant Manual.*
CDs: *Wakey Wakey, Praying from His Heart, Positioning for Transition, Keeping His Peace, Wellness Seminar* (on bethel.tv).
ibethel.org, and bethel.tv

Ray Hughes: *Sound of Heaven Symphony of Earth.*
CDs: *The Warhorse, The Song of David, The Minstrel Series, The Tabernacle of David.*
selahministries.com

Danny Silk: *Culture of Honor, Keep Your Love On, Powerful and Free: Confronting the Glass Ceiling For Women in the Church, Loving Our Kids on Purpose* (the DVD version of this is amazing).
CDs/DVDs: *"Loving on Purpose Leadership Series, Unpunishable, Honor among Us, Loving on Purpose Relationship Series, Loving Our Kids on Purpose.*
lovingonpurpose.com and ibethel.org

Patricia King: *Decree, Tongues, Light Belongs in the Darkness: Finding Your Place in God's Endtime Harvest.*
CDs: *Tongues, The Glory School, Spiritual Cleanse, Decree for Kids, Psalm 23 for Kids.*
xpmedia.com

Kris Vallotton: *The Supernatural Ways of Royalty* (with Bill Johnson), *Spirit Wars, Basic Training in the Prophetic, Developing a Supernatural Lifestyle, Moral Revolution.*
CDs: *Fashioned to Reign, Identity Series Flash Drive, Prophetic Series Flash Drive, God's Most Beautiful Creation.*
ibethel.org and bethel.tv

Randy Clark: *Ministry Team Training, Open Heaven: Are You Thirsty, Essential Guide to Healing* (with Bill Johnson), *Pressing In: Spend and Be Spent, Healing Unplugged* (with Bill Johnson).
globalawakening.com

Sheri Silk: CDs: *Insert Love Here, The Test of Honor, To Be Known, When Your Process Meets Your Destiny.*
lovingonpurpose.com and ibethel.org

Steve Backlund: *Igniting Faith in 40 Days, Cracks in the Foundation, Possessing Joy, Why We Make Declarations.*
CDs: *Relentless Mind Renewal, Framing Our Future.*
ignitinghope.com

Dann Farrelly: CD: *Brave Communication.*
ibethel.org

Heidi Baker: *Compelled by Love, Learning to Love, The Hungry Always Get Fed* (with Rolland Baker), *There Is Always Enough* (with Rolland Baker), *Birthing the Miraculous.*
CDs: *Stopping for Someone Every Day, Love Must Look Like Something, Learning to Love, Fully Satisfied and Ravenously Hungry.*
irisglobal.org

Banning Liebscher: *Journey of a World Changer, Jesus Culture: Living a Life That Transforms the World, Revival Culture"* (with Michael Brodeur).
CDs: *It's Time to Go Public, The Now Breed of Revivalist," Foundation of a Revivalist, Jesus Culture Encounter.*
new.jesusculture.com and ibethel.org

Iverna Tompkins: *God's Ravished Heart, If It Please the King.*
CDs: *Enlarging Your Tent, Foundations for Spiritual Growth, What Is Your Problem* (1&2), *Women on the Frontlines.*
ivernainternational.com

Judy Franklin: *Experiencing the Heavenly Realm: Keys to Accessing Supernatural Experiences* (with Beni Johnson), *The Physics of Heaven, Heaven Can't Wait.*
CD: *His Love.*
heavensphysics.com and ibethel.org

Dan McCollam: *Basic Training in the Prophetic, God Vibrations Study Guide.*
CDs: *Living on the Right Side of the Cross, Worship at the Next Level, Unlocking Your Dreams, Anachronistic Living, Heavenly Realms, God Vibrations, Encouragement.*
imissionchurch.com

Bobby Conner: *God's Supernatural Power, Shepherd's Rod.*
CDs: *Open Heaven 2013* (with Bob Hartley), *Revelation of Love.*
bobbyconnor.org and ibethel.org

Don Potter: *Facing the Wall, Things I Thought I Knew.*
Music: *Come up Here, Now Is the Time to Return.*
potterhausmusic.net

Arthur Burk: *Blessing Your Spirit.*
CDs: *Developing Your Spirit, Nurturing Your Spirit* (I, II, & III).
theslg.com

Dawna De Silva & Teresa Liebscher: *SOZO Basic* and *SOZO Advanced* (Saved, Healed and Delivered).
ibethel.org

Sue Elliott: *SOZO Children.*
ibethel.org

John & Carol Arnott: *Grace and Forgiveness.*
catchthefire.com

John Paul Jackson: *Breaking Free of Rejection.*
streamsministries.com

Kevin Dedmon: *Fire Starters, TNT, Treasure Hunt.*
kevindedmon.com

Kathie Walters: *Prophetic Seer* (6-book set).
CDs: The Fanatic in the Attic, Getting Free from Religious Spirits, Faith and Angels.
kathiewaltersministry.com

Bob Johnson: *Love Stains.*
CDs: *Orphan Heart, The Chase, True Sonship.*
ibethel.org

James Goll: *The Lost Art of Worship, The Seer Expanded Edition, Deliverance from Darkness, The Prophetic Intercessor.*
encountersnetwork.com

Wesley & Stacey Campbell: *Praying the Bible: The Book of Prayers, Praying the Bible: The Pathway to Spirituality.*
revivalnow.com

Eric Johnson: *Momentum.*
CDs: *Get Your Own Milk, Create, Moving from Inheritance to Responsibility, Ideas, Out of the Box, Creating Powerful People, Jesus Never Promoted Himself.*
ibethel.org

Doug Addison: *Spiritual Identity Theft Exposed, Personal Development God's Way.*
dougaddison.com

Bob Hartley: *The Two Spies, Adoration.*
CD: *Heart of Adoration.*
bobhartley.org

Joaquin Evans: *Enjoying the Process, Maturing into Childlikeness, Living with Supernatural Expectancy, Healing for the Nations.*
ibethel.org

Misty Edwards: *What Is the Point.*
Music: *Fling Wide, Only a Shadow, Relentless.*
mistyedwards.com and ihopkc.org

Seth Dahl: CD: *Undercover & In The Flow; Out of Striving, Into Rest.*

Mike Bickle: *After God's Own Heart, Passion for Jesus.*
mikebickle.org and ihopkc.org

Bethel Church: *Cultivating the Presence, Inspire, What If, Lovely* (women's conf.), *School of Worship, School of Healing, School of Evangelism.*
ibethel.org and bethel.tv

Worship and Soaking Music:

Jason Upton, Alberto & Kimberly Rivera, JoAnn McFatter, Julie Meyer, Bethel Music, Jesus Culture, Steve Swanson, Kim Walker-Smith, Jonathan David Helser, Brian & Jenn Johnson, Jeremy Riddle, Nic & Rachael Billman, Misty Edwards, Brian & Katie Torwalt, Hillsong United, Amber Brooks, Joshua Mills, Leah Mari, Rebekah Van Tinteren, Faith Blatchford, Georgian & Winnie Banov, Leonard Jones, Kathi Oates.

In case you are wondering, yes, the bread crumbs do keep coming. There is nothing on the planet that compares to the experience or the enjoyment of knowing God.